—

Amazing

CLEVER
TRICKS

Magic and more to
astound your friends!

LORENZ BOOKS

First published in 2000 by Lorenz Books

LORENZ BOOKS are available for bulk purchase for sales
promotion and for premium use. For details, write or call the
sales director, Lorenz Books, 27 West 20th Street, New York,
NY 10011; (800) 354-9657

Lorenz Books is an imprint of
Anness Publishing Limited

ISBN 0 7548 0238 8

Publisher: Joanna Lorenz
Managing Editor, Children's Books: Gilly Cameron-Cooper
Senior Editor: Nicole Pearson
Editorial Assistant: Jenni Rainford
Photography: John Freeman, Tim Ridley
Design: Caroline Grimshaw

Previously published as part of the following larger
compendiums:
The Outrageously Big Activity, Play and Project Book, *The Ultimate
Show-Me-How Activity Book* and *The Really Big Book of Amazing
Things to Make and Do*

Printed in Hong Kong/China

10 9 8 7 6 5 4 3 2 1

Foreword

If you like clowning around and doing magic tricks, then look no further! In here you'll find great ideas for amazing magic tricks, balloon art and juggling to stun your family and friends. Detailed step-by-step instructions show you how to create fun, funky models from just a few balloons. You'll also learn how to juggle bean bags—or bananas! There are plenty of magic tricks to learn, from the Coin Through Hand trick that needs no preparation, to the Time-bomb Escape, which is as much fun to set up as it is to perform. You'll also learn lots of hot tips on how to put on a really good show with plenty of razzmatazz. So put on your performer's biggest smile and get ready to take the stage!

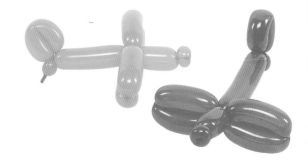

Contents

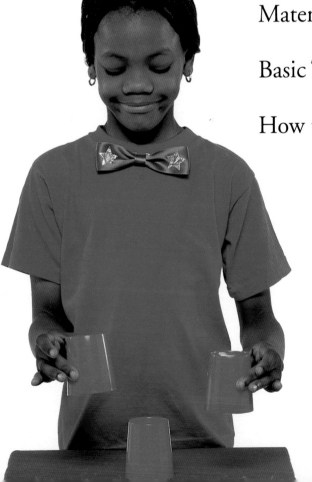

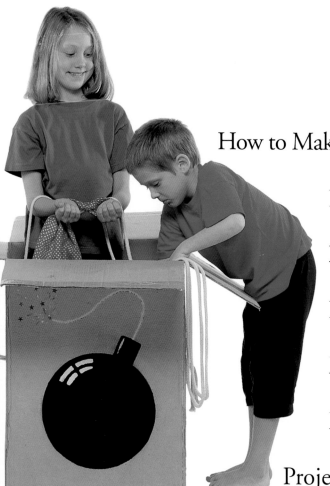

A Magic Show

Hugh Nightingale

Introduction

So, you want to be a magician? Good! Because magic is fun. Actually, it is *great* fun. Making the tricks is fun, doing the tricks is fun and, most of all, entertaining people with magic is fun.

Some people, and books, say magic is very hard to do because it needs hour after hour, year after year, of never-ending practice. Well, in this chapter you will find lots of tricks that you will be able to do easily with only a little practice. And once you've learned how to do all the projects shown here, you might go on to learn the more complicated secrets of magic.

Making Things for Your Magic

The Wand

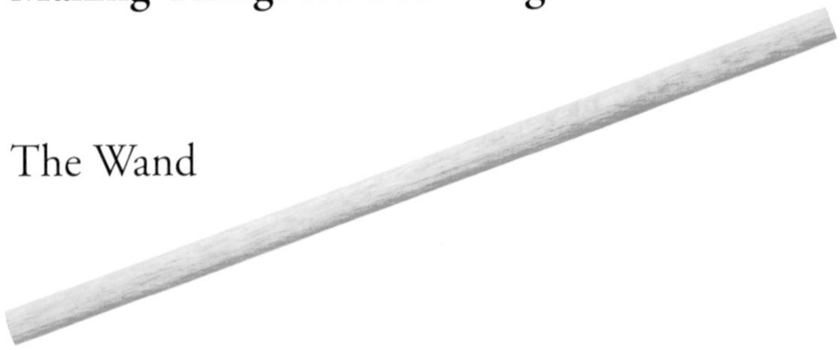

In order to practice magic, you need a few essential props. The most important of these is your wand. You can make one yourself. All you need is a 12 in length of round wood, called a dowel, some masking tape and black and white paints. Wrap masking tape around each end of the dowel and paint the wood in-between black. When the paint is dry, remove the tape and paint the ends white. Presto! The stick has magically become a wand, ready for you to do some brilliant tricks with.

The Magic Box

An essential prop is a beautifully colored magic box. This box means you will be able to produce many things you need for your show, out of a box that seems to be empty!

1 First tape over the sharp edges of an empty 850 g baked bean can. Then glue a rectangle of red card together at the edges, to make a tube wider and taller than the can. For the outer box, join four identical pieces of stiff cardboard with masking tape. Ask a grown-up to help you cut out some holes in one piece for the front of the box.

2 Here Lucy has decorated the box to look like an old-fashioned radio. Now paint half of the bean can and the inside of the box with black poster paint. When the paint is dry, fill the tin with magical things.

3 Put the bean can, filled with silk handkerchiefs, cards, a small pink rabbit and a plastic fried egg, inside the box. Can you see it? No? That is because you place it in the box with its black side facing the holes in the front, so when you lift out the red tube the box appears empty. After putting the red tube back over the bean can, you can lift up the radio box, because it has no bottom, to show that it is empty as well.

4 This "illusion" means that Lucy can produce the hankies, cards and rabbit from an "empty" box. She can turn the can around when it is inside the tube and lift it out, with the egg, to add a funny finish to her trick. Now, once she has put the can and egg away, she can again show her audience that the tube and box are both empty.

This time, as there is nothing left to hide, she can hold the tube and box up together.

The Hat

Every self-respecting magician has a top hat, and it is needed for many of the tricks in this book.

1 Ask a friend to measure around your head. Add 1 in to the figure and cut a piece of stiff black paper to this length, about 6 in wide. Roll the paper into a tube and glue the edges together.

2 For the top of the hat, place the tube upright on a sheet of black paper and draw around it with a white crayon. Draw a second circle about ½ in wider around the first circle and cut out the outer line. Cut small "V"s around the whole shape between the outer and inner circles. Glue the tabs downward inside the top of the tube. To make the brim, draw around the shape of your hat onto more black paper. Draw a second circle ½ in smaller than your tube and a third circle 2½ in larger. Cut out along these last two lines. Cut tabs again and glue them into the bottom of your hat.

3 A secret flap fixed inside your magician's top hat is perfect for hiding things. Cut out a round piece of stiff black paper to fit snugly into the hat. Tape a flap onto the middle of it with masking tape. Paint the tape black and cut the flap into a semicircle so that it can be held against either side of the hat, with your fingers. If you briefly tip the opening of the hat toward the audience, anything hidden behind the flap will not be seen. They will see just blackness inside the hat and assume the hat is empty.

4 Add some ribbon to the hat to finish it off. Measure around the tube of your hat, and add ½ in to this. Glue the ribbon around the hat just above the brim with a ½ in overlap. A black or colored bow tie will make you really look like a magician.

Performing

Performing magic is all about acting the part of the magician convincingly. When you are doing a trick, you must try to believe that magic is really happening. If you believe it, so will your audience.

What to Say

What you say to your audience during your show is called your patter. The most important thing is to be natural. Talk in your own way. Make up a story to go with the trick and add a few jokes if you would like to get a laugh.

Repeating Tricks

When you have done a good trick, people will ask to see it again. Don't be tempted to repeat it! Your audience might discover the secret of the trick the second time around.

Misdirection

This is the art of making your audience look where *you* want them to look. The audience will look where your eyes are looking or at your moving hands. If you are hiding a coin in your hand, don't look at that hand. Also, never say that a box or hat is "empty" or the audience will be suspicious. Quickly show them the inside and they will assume that it is empty.

Secrets

Always keep your magic secrets to yourself. Store your magic things out of sight, in a case or a closed box.

Appearance

Look smart and especially have clean hands and fingernails. Smile. Look happy. If you feel a little shy in front of an audience, try your tricks out in private first, and even in front of a mirror.

Mistakes

Sometimes things will go wrong (even the most famous magicians sometimes make mistakes!). Don't panic. If you can, correct things and carry on. If you can't, just smile and get the audience involved in another trick. Remember that your audience is there because they want to be entertained and they want you to do well. Practicing your tricks in front of a mirror will help prevent the mistakes from happening.

Magic Secrets

Part of the skill of being a magician is keeping things to yourself. In order to show how to do things, we have taken photographs, but whenever you see the top hat symbol, this is a view that the audience should not see.

How Many Tricks?

Don't make your show too long. That way you will leave your audience wanting more and they will ask you for another show on another day. Plan a short show that has a beginning, a middle and an end. And don't forget – smile!

Magic Words

In magic there are many special words. Here are some useful ones for you to learn.

EFFECT   What the audience sees.

GAG   A joke or a funny story.

GIMMICK OR FAKE   A secret part of the prop that the audience does not see.

ILLUSION   When something *seems* to happen but doesn't.

LOAD   The things held in a secret compartment.

PALMING   Keeping something hidden in your hand.

PATTER   Your talk that goes with the trick.

PRODUCTION   Making something appear from nowhere.

PROPS   The things you use for your tricks.

ROUTINE   A series of tricks or moves.

SHUFFLE   To mix up cards in your hands.

SILKS   Silk handkerchiefs.

SLEEVING   Hiding something up your sleeve to make it vanish or ready to appear in your hand later.

SLEIGHT OF HAND   A clever movement of your hand to make magic.

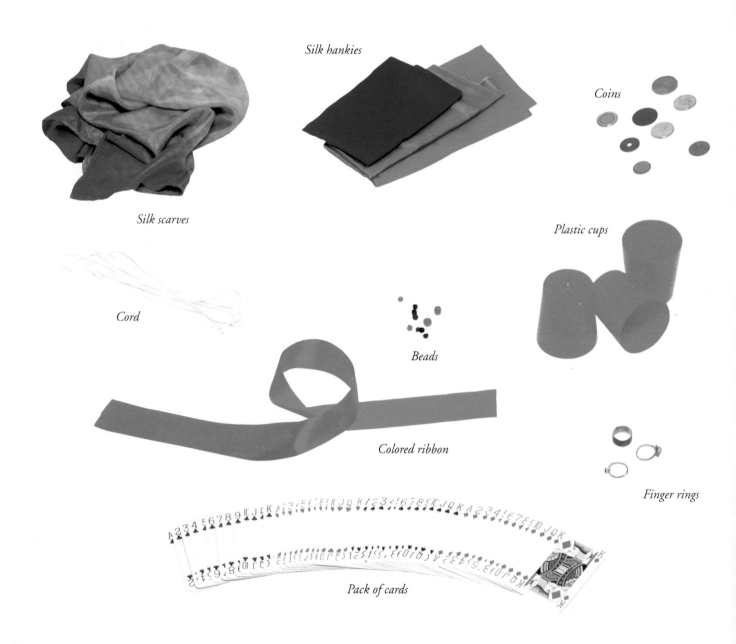

Silk hankies

Coins

Silk scarves

Plastic cups

Cord

Beads

Colored ribbon

Finger rings

Pack of cards

STEAL To move something from its place secretly.

SWITCH To change one thing for another secretly.

TALK The sound that hidden objects might make – for example, rattle, click, etc.

TRANSPOSITION When something magically disappears from one place to reappear in another.

VANISH To make an object seem to disappear.

Materials

The materials that you will need are always listed. Gather them all together before you start. Work on a suitable surface. Wear an apron if you are painting or gluing, and put everything away afterward. Allow time for paint and glue to dry before moving onto the next stage. Keep a collection of empty cartons, tubes and boxes, etc. Once they have been painted and decorated they are great for magic. Take great care when using scissors or other sharp instruments, and always ask a grown-up to help if you need to use a craft knife.

Black is a very useful color in magic because a black object in black surroundings becomes almost invisible. So, if the instructions for a trick say to use black, then *do* use black. Finally, take your time and study the photographs and the text carefully. If a photograph shows someone doing a trick with her right hand and you prefer to use your left, don't worry. Just switch things around and do it your own way.

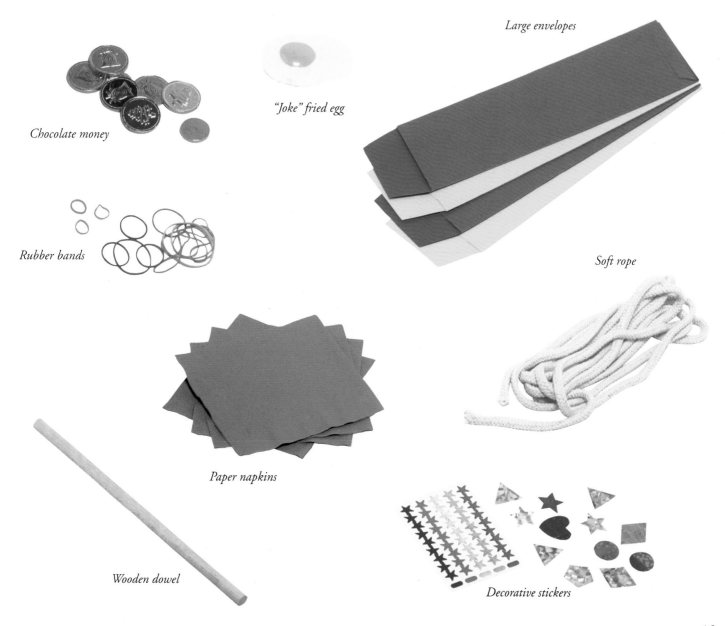

Large envelopes

"Joke" fried egg

Chocolate money

Rubber bands

Soft rope

Paper napkins

Wooden dowel

Decorative stickers

The Dirty Napkin Trick

Magic can have the most powerful effect when people are not expecting it. Here's a trick you could do during a meal. Sarah has this trick well under control. When the person opposite her has sat down and spread his paper napkin on his knee, she asks him for the napkin. She gives the excuse that she has noticed some tiny stains on it. To do the trick she tears off pieces from the center of the napkin, explaining each time that "this one's gravy, this one's ketchup," and so on. Finally she opens up the napkin to show that it is whole – without any bits torn out of it. This trick is a real reputation maker. Try it yourself.

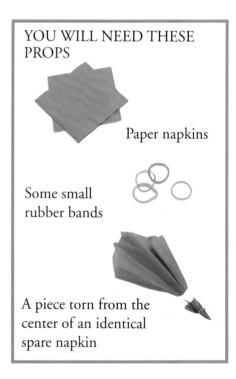

YOU WILL NEED THESE PROPS

Paper napkins

Some small rubber bands

A piece torn from the center of an identical spare napkin

Tip

Don't use your own napkin for the secret torn piece, as someone might ask to see it afterwards. When you tear off the pieces, remove the rubber band with one of them (see step 6).

1 Secretly, under the table, attach the torn piece of napkin to the inside of your left thumb with the rubber band, so that it is hidden in your hand.

2 Borrow a napkin from another diner. Nobody will notice the torn piece as you reach across the table to take the napkin.

3 Spread the napkin over your left hand and point to the "stains" as you push the center of the napkin into your hand.

4 The real center, and the torn center, are side by side. Here we can see under Sarah's napkin, but don't let anyone else see what is happening.

5 Take both the centers into your right hand. Turn them upside down and put them back into your left hand. Pull up only the torn piece.

6 Tear off pieces, saying they are stained, and put them in your pocket. Remove the rubber band with one of the pieces.

7 Really, you are tearing pieces from the extra piece in your hand. It will look as if you are tearing them from the center of the napkin.

8 When it looks as though you have thoroughly ruined the napkin, calmly open up the real napkin to the amazement of everyone.

Money from Nowhere!

How about this for a trick? You are holding your empty top hat in one hand, then, with the other hand, you reach up and pluck a gold coin out of the air and drop it into your hat. Then you find another in the air, then another and another. Aribibia is finding coins all over the place, even behind people's ears! Finally he tips his hat onto the table and out pours a shower of golden coins. There are enough coins to hand out to friends after the show. When you do this trick, you will use a specially prepared coin, so make sure you do not give it away but keep it safely for next time.

YOU WILL NEED THESE PROPS

Sticking plaster

Scissors

Chocolate money

Your top hat, with the flap

Tip
For your special coin, to save it melting, carefully take the chocolate out of the foil and make it vanish, in your mouth! Replace it with a disk of cardboard and you can use the coin over and over again.

16

1 Before you start the trick, attach about 2 in of sticking plaster to one side of your special coin, leaving about 1 in hanging free.

2 Load one side of your hat flap with chocolate money. With the flap over the money, you can show your audience that the hat is "empty."

3 Hold the coin between your finger and thumb with the plaster stuck to your second and third fingers. Keep the back of your hand to the audience.

4 Hold your hand over the hat, and let the coin go. It will fall behind your fingers, but the audience will believe it has fallen into the hat.

5 Flick the coin up again, and catch it with your thumb. You've caught a coin from the air! Drop it into the hat. Repeat this action several times.

6 Shake the hat to rattle the coins that are already in it. The audience will be convinced that you have caught a hatful of coins from thin air.

7 Finally pour the coins onto the table to show just how many you have collected from thin air.

Magic Wands

It always looks good, in your show, to wave your wand whenever you wish the "magic" to happen. Nhat Han has also discovered some tricks that use the wand itself. She can make the wand "magnetic"; it will cling to her hand with, apparently, nothing holding it in place. She can, or so it appears, push the wand right into her leg and it doesn't hurt her. She can also make her wand stiff one minute and bendy the next. How does she do that?

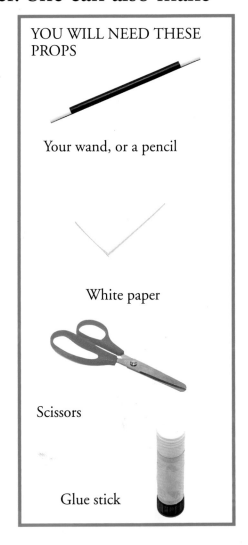

YOU WILL NEED THESE PROPS

Your wand, or a pencil

White paper

Scissors

Glue stick

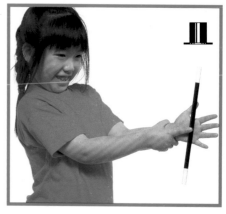

Magnetic Wand

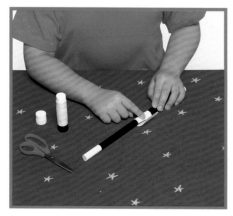

1 If you are holding a wand and you open your hand, it falls to the floor. Oh, dear!

2 But if you are a magician, like Nhat Han, it will stay in your hand all by itself.

3 Look on the other side of her hand. Can you see her secret? Try it yourself.

Painless Wand

1 Nhat Han rolls up a piece of white paper and glues it to make a tube the same size as the tip of her wand.

2 Nhat Han has pushed the wand right into her leg! But it did not seem to hurt! How did she do that?

3 She hid the lower wand tip in her hand and pushed the paper tube down the wand with her other hand.

Wobbly Wand

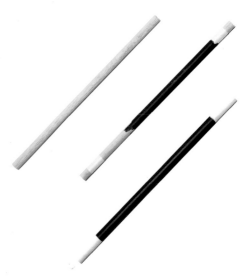

1 Nhat Han is trying to bend her wand. It is definitely stiff.

2 Next, she holds it loosely between finger and thumb, about one-third of the way down. When she moves it from side to side, it looks wobbly.

The Coin Fold

Tricks with money always get the audience's attention, especially if you make the money disappear and it belongs to someone in the audience! Alexander finds that the coin fold shown here is a very useful method for helping to make a coin vanish easily. But he had to practice hard to perfect his technique, especially making the coin reappear from Michelle's ear.

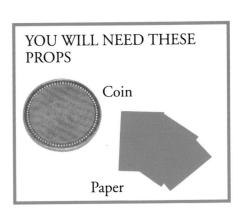

YOU WILL NEED THESE PROPS

Coin

Paper

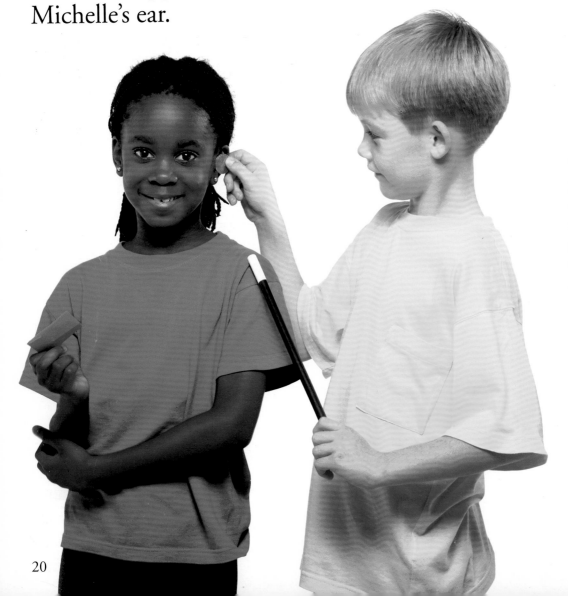

Tip
Because the viewers see you wrap the coin in the paper, their eyes stay on the paper packet. This "misdirection" allows you to drop the coin into your hand.

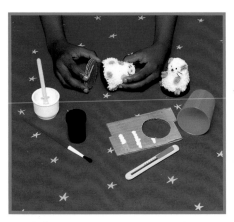

1 Ask a grown-up to cut out three circles to just fit inside a beaker. Paint them black. Leave to dry, then glue the circles onto the three mice.

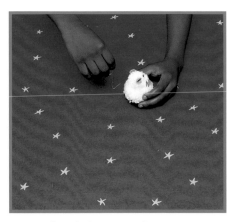

2 Unbend the paper clip to make a hook at each end. Push one end into the fourth mouse. Hook it to your back before starting the trick.

3 Practice lifting up a beaker with a mouse inside. If you squeeze the cup when you lift it, the mouse stays in the cup and seems to "disappear."

4 Now for the performance. Arrange three beakers, each with a mouse hidden inside, in a line. Show the audience only the middle mouse.

5 Squeeze the two end beakers gently as you lift them (to hold the mice inside) to show they are "empty."

6 Swap the two end beakers with the middle one. Then lift the new middle beaker to show that the mouse has magically jumped back.

7 Swap the beakers again. Take the mouse from the end cup and put it in your top hat. Lift the middle cup. The mouse has "jumped" back again!

8 Repeat until all the mice are in the hat, then show that the hat is also "empty." The audience will see where the mouse is when you turn around!

Postman's Wand

Gerald is demonstrating a really smart trick he has learned. He puts his wand into an envelope, ready to post it. Then he performs a little magic, and Alakazam! The wand disappears from the envelope and then reappears in a different envelope on the other side of the room.

Tips

Find some large envelopes that fit your wand, in different colors if possible or decorate them differently.

Make sure the envelopes stay in view at all times. Prop them up against the backs of two chairs if necessary.

Before you put the wand into the envelope, tap the chairs or tables with the wand. This proves that the wand is solid without your actually having to say so, which would seem suspicious.

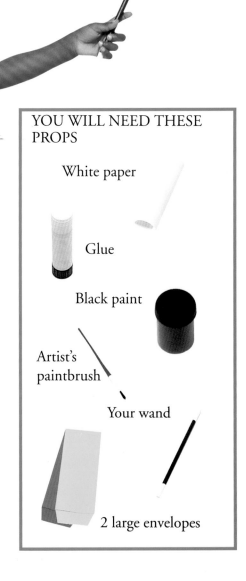

YOU WILL NEED THESE PROPS

White paper

Glue

Black paint

Artist's paintbrush

Your wand

2 large envelopes

1 Roll up some paper and glue it to make a hollow paper wand. Paint it to look like a real wand. When the paint is dry, slide it over the real wand.

2 Show your audience the two empty envelopes and place them apart on two tables or chairs.

3 Put the wand into one envelope. Shake your head and take it out, secretly letting the real wand slide out of the paper one into the envelope.

4 Put the paper wand into the other envelope, saying, "I prefer it in this one." Now the trick is done, but the audience thinks it has just started.

5 So now it is all acting. Make a magical "switching over" sign with your arms.

6 The audience saw you put the wand in the second envelope yet you can prove it is now empty by scrunching it up into a ball.

7 With a grand gesture, open up the first envelope to reveal your real wand, which has magically traveled through the air. Magician, take a bow.

Back-flip Card

Tip
When someone has chosen a card, ask them to show it to someone else (not you!). This helps to prevent their forgetting which card they chose, which would spoil the trick.

When people know you do magic, they will often ask to see a card trick. The trouble is, many card tricks involve complicated, finger-twisting moves. But try this: if you can put a pack of cards behind your back, turn the whole pack over and then turn just the top card over, you can do this trick. It is that easy. You have to have a reason for putting the cards behind your back, so explain that anyone can do a card trick when they can see the cards, but it takes a *real* magician to do it behind their back. Here, Michelle tries the trick out on Alexander.

YOU WILL NEED THESE PROPS

Pack of cards

1 Shuffle the cards, then hold them like a fan, facedown in your hand. Ask a friend to take a card and remember it, but not to let you see it.

2 While talking about doing tricks behind your back, put the pack behind your back and turn it over. Pick off the top card.

3 Turn this card over and put it back on top of the pack. Do this quite quickly. Then bring the cards to the front again.

4 Hold the cards as a pack. All the cards are faceup except the top one. Ask your friend to slide his card into the pack; keep the pack closed.

5 Put the pack behind your back again and pick off the top card.

6 Turn over the top card and put it back on the pack. Then turn the whole pack over while you say you are trying to find your friend's card.

7 Bring the pack to the front again and spread them out. Hocus-pocus! One card is faceup, and yes – it is the very card that was chosen!

Coin Through Hand

An impromptu trick is one that you can do anywhere with no preparation or "props." All you need for this impromptu trick is your hands and a coin, which you can borrow. It is also very easy to do and is the first coin trick real magicians usually learn. You can really "act" this one. The audience members, at first, think they have caught you out, so they are even more surprised when the coin really does end up in your fist. Michael shows us how to do it.

YOU WILL NEED THESE PROPS

Coin

Tip
Use a medium to large coin, if possible. Small, light coins sometimes stick to your fingers and do not drop when you want them to.

1 Hold the coin above your left fist, as shown, and announce, "I'm going to push this coin through the back of my hand."

2 As you push the coin down, it slides up, out of sight behind your fingers. "There, it's gone through," you can say.

3 Open your fist and say, "Whoops! It must have got stuck, halfway." The audience members, though, think they know where it is.

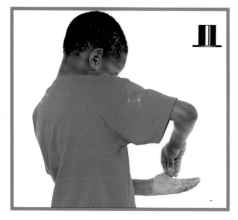

4 "I'll try again," you say as you do the sneaky part. The sneaky part is that, as you turn your left hand back over into a fist, your thumb almost brushes against the tips of the fingers holding the coin. Just at this point you let the coin slip out of your fingers, and you catch it in your left hand, which you make into a fist.

5 It all happens so quickly the audience members believe it is still hidden behind your fingers. You say, "I'll give it a harder push this time."

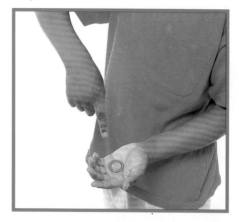

6 Now slowly turn your fist over and open it up. "Ah, there it is!"

Purple Hanky, Red Hanky

People in the audience love to come up and help during a show. For this trick, two assistants are needed. Nicola cleverly chose Scott, who was wearing a purple T-shirt, to hold the wrapped purple silk hanky, and Tope, who was wearing red, to hold the wrapped red silk hanky. Scott and Tope never let go of their packages, but Nicola makes them keep changing sides. A wave of her wand and, Presto! The hankies have changed places. Now, that *is* magic! How is it done? Well, the newspapers are not as ordinary as they seem.

Tips

If you choose volunteers who are wearing the same colors as your silk handkerchiefs, it is easier for the audience to follow the trick and for you to remember where the different silks are all the time.

When you tear open the package at the end of the trick, take care not to tear too deeply or you will expose the wrong silk.

YOU WILL NEED THESE PROPS

2 pairs of silk hankies in contrasting colors, such as red and purple

Newspaper

Glue stick

Tape

Your wand

1 Before the show, lay out a silk handkerchief on a sheet of newspaper and spread glue around it (not on it!) with the glue stick.

2 Stick a second sheet on top. Do the same with a silk in the other color. Make a secret mark on the papers, so you know which is which.

3 Fold up the sheets of newspapers and put them on your table, with your wand and the tape. Show the audience the remaining two silks.

4 Wrap the red silk in the paper which has the purple one hidden inside, and make a rough ball shape.

5 Use tape to hold the package together. Now wrap the purple silk in the paper with the red one inside, and hold it together with tape.

6 Ask for two volunteers. Give the wrapped red silk to someone wearing red and the wrapped purple silk to someone in purple.

7 Ask your volunteers to swap places while holding onto their packages. Wave your wand in the air to make the magic work.

8 Tear open the outer layer of the "purple" package. Instead of a purple silk, you pull out a red one! And from the "red" you pull out a purple silk.

33

X-ray Wand and Ringing Up

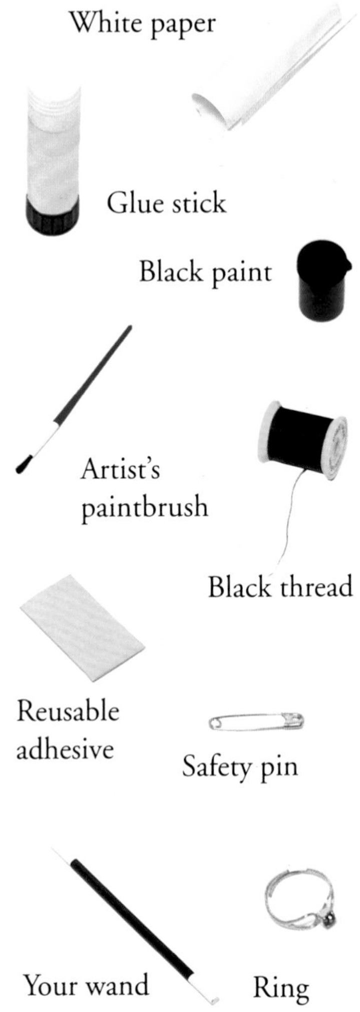

Here are two special tricks using magic wands, but with a difference. The second trick uses your wooden wand, but the first one uses a hollow wand. Carl has made a hollow wand by rolling up a sheet of paper and painting it to look like a real one. The X-ray Wand routine is perfect for when you are showing a trick to just one friend, because you actually teach them how to do it. They will be amazed to see a hole right through their hand. Ringing Up is great fun because you can use a ring that you have borrowed from someone in the audience. People always enjoy seeing their own things behaving in strange magical ways.

YOU WILL NEED THESE PROPS

White paper

Glue stick

Black paint

Artist's paintbrush

Black thread

Reusable adhesive

Safety pin

Your wand

Ring

Clowning Around

Nick Huckleberry Beak

Introduction

So you want to throw things around and catch them again? Create animals out of thin air and rubber? Generally clown around and have fun? Well, you have come to the right place because this is all about juggling and crazy balloon modeling. But be warned—juggling fever is catching and balloon modeling can make your day end with a bang!

Juggling fun

Once you have learned the basics of juggling there is no turning back. You will start with balloon balls and bean bags, then you will want to juggle fruit, plates, cups, sneakers and small pieces of furniture. Before you know it you will be doing Under or Over juggling with the family pet, the Statue of Liberty and an elephant. Nothing is safe—everything can be juggled. Some of the juggling moves are really easy and you will catch on (ha! ha!) in a flash. Other juggling routines will take

practice, patience and a bit more practice. If you do not have juggling balls, do not worry—there are instructions for making your own balloon balls and bean bags. But if you just cannot wait to start juggling, you can practice with scarves, fruit (ask permission first) or even socks partially filled with uncooked rice. (Cooked rice is impossible to juggle with!) Do not try juggling priceless pieces of china or expensive electronic equipment—just yet!

Balloon modeling bug

Twist, twist, bend, bend, stretch, twist and pop! No, this is not a new dance or a new breakfast cereal. This is the sound of someone with the balloon modeling bug. The good thing about this bug is that it is fun to pass it on! Without so much as a huff or a puff, you will be able to create a world of hairless dogs, featherless birds and flowers that survive without water. You will even be able to build a light-filled, airy house with nothing more than 17 balloons and a balloon pump.

To start, you will make models for yourself, then you will perform feats of balloon magic at parties, fairs and carnivals. But once the bug has really taken hold you will be balloon modeling while waiting for the bus, during school and under your blanket at night. It is not that you have gone mad, you have simply become a balloonatic!

This is how all new jugglers look—cross-eyed and confused!

This is the look of someone who has caught juggling fever and is having a great time.

This is a balloonatic. Her balloon modeling skills have gone totally to her head.

Materials

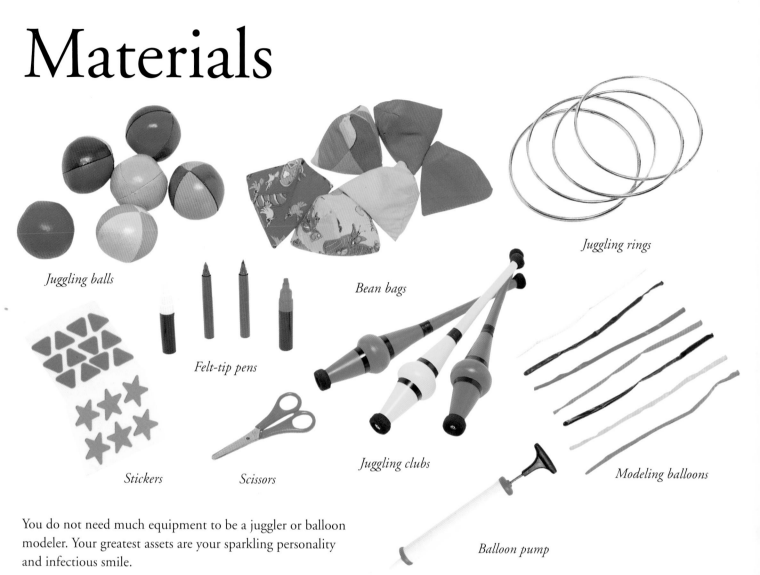

Juggling balls

Bean bags

Juggling rings

Felt-tip pens

Stickers

Scissors

Juggling clubs

Modeling balloons

Balloon pump

You do not need much equipment to be a juggler or balloon modeler. Your greatest assets are your sparkling personality and infectious smile.

Balloon pump There are many types of balloon pumps available, but you must make sure that you get one with a tapered nozzle on the end. These are specially made to inflate modeling balloons. The most effective type of pump is a double-action pump. This pump inflates the balloon when you push the pump in and when you pull it out.

Bean bags These are made from cotton fabric and shaped like pyramids. They are often filled with dried beans. You can buy them at joke stores and theatrical supply stores, or you can make your own. You will need three or more bean bags.

Felt-tip pens To decorate and draw faces onto your balloon modeling creations, you will need indelible felt-tip pens. Indelible means that your drawings will not rub off the smooth surface of the balloon.

Juggling balls These are soft, plastic-covered balls that come in lots of bright colors and patterns. You can buy inexpensive sets of juggling balls at toy and joke stores, or make your own using round party balloons and uncooked rice.

Juggling clubs These can be bought in sets or separately, and they come in various sizes. They are quite expensive. Instead of clubs, try your juggling moves with plastic bowling pins. You can even decorate the pins to look just like the real thing.

Juggling rings When you become very confident at juggling, you could buy a set of juggling rings. They are made of metal and come in various sizes.

Modeling balloons These are long, thin balloons that come in a variety of colors. You can buy them in bags of 100 at toy and hobby stores, and also at specialty theatrical suppliers. All the balloons used in these projects are the "260" type. Modeling balloons can lose some of their quality over time, and are best kept in a cool, dark place.

Scissors You will need a pair of scissors to cut balloons to make balloon balls, to make bean bags and to do one of the tricks.

Stickers You can use stickers to decorate balloon models and juggling equipment. Buy sheets of plain colored or fancy stickers at toy and stationery stores.

Basic Techniques

Inflating modeling balloons and tying knots

Modeling balloons are easier to inflate and less likely to burst if they are warm. You can warm them by stretching them a few times and by keeping them out of the refrigerator. Do not leave balloons in sunlight—this will speed up the process of disintegration.

Bang! Some balloons are (pop! burst!) weaker than others. On average, about one in every 25 to 30 balloons bursts during inflating, so do not (bang!) worry—it is not your fault. Immediately discard the burst balloon and any small pieces that have fallen on the floor by putting them in the wastebasket or out of reach of young children and pets.

The only trick to tying a knot in a modeling balloon is patience. If you take it slowly and keep a tight grip on the balloon, the balloon will be tied in knots, not you!

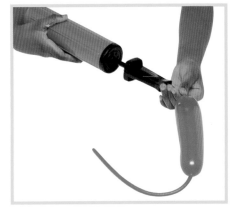

1 **Inflating the balloon**—carefully insert the nozzle of the balloon pump into the mouth of the balloon about 3/4 in. Hold the balloon in place. If you let go of the balloon while it is being inflated, you can easily imagine what happens.

2 Start inflating your balloon, but always leave an uninflated bit at the end. This is important, as each time you twist the inflated balloon air will be forced down the balloon. The more twists used to create a model, the longer the uninflated end should be.

3 **Tying a knot**—this is often the cause of much frustration, but really it is not difficult. Hold the end of the mouth of the balloon tightly to keep it sealed. Then stretch the neck of the balloon around two fingers, as shown. Do not pull too tightly—it hurts. Ouch!

4 Pull on the end of the balloon until it crosses the neck of the balloon and the two fingers. Hold with the thumb.

5 Tuck the end of the balloon down between the two fingers and through the circle—in other words, tie a knot!

6 Keeping hold of the end, slip your fingers out of the knot and pull it tight. Phew!

Decorating your balloon models

You can make your balloon models more colorful, realistic or comical by drawing on them or decorating them.

The simplest and quickest way to decorate balloons is to use indelible felt-tip pens. As well as using a variety of bright colors, get hold of a white pen if possible. White is really effective when drawing eyes, as it makes them stand out.

Eyes, a nose and mouth are probably the first things you will want to give your animal balloon models. Why not also draw on paws, feathers or fur, or just wild and wonderful patterns? You could give Pampered Pooch, for example, a fancy collar and name tag. If you are making a model for a friend, you could write their name or a message on it. A balloon model elephant that says "Happy Birthday" on one side would make a very unusual birthday card.

You can also use small stickers to decorate your models. Stickers come in lots of different shapes, textures and colors. There are even sticker packs of eyes, noses, ears and other facial features. Once your sticker is in position, you will not be able to remove it without bursting the balloon.

To apply paint to a balloon model, you first have to mix white glue into the paint before you apply it. The white glue will make the paint stick to the balloon. Apply the paint gently and use a soft brush.

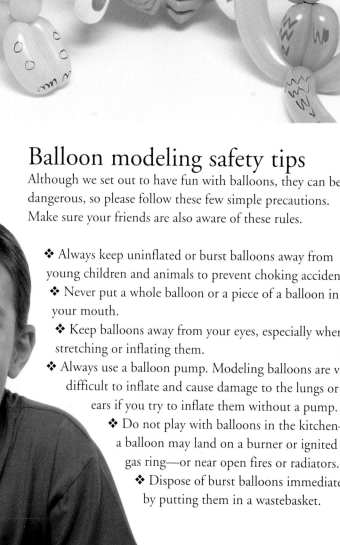

Juggling safety tips

❖ Do not attempt to juggle with sharp or pointed utensils or heavy objects. Sharp things will cut you, and heavy objects will give you a nasty bump on your head or will land slap, bang, ouch on your little toe!
❖ Make sure you have lots of room around you and above you when juggling. Ask an adult to move furniture out of the way so that you do not trip over it. Breakable items should be moved to another country for safekeeping!

Just as well this girl was only juggling balloon balls!

Balloon modeling safety tips

Although we set out to have fun with balloons, they can be dangerous, so please follow these few simple precautions. Make sure your friends are also aware of these rules.

❖ Always keep uninflated or burst balloons away from young children and animals to prevent choking accidents.
❖ Never put a whole balloon or a piece of a balloon in your mouth.
❖ Keep balloons away from your eyes, especially when stretching or inflating them.
❖ Always use a balloon pump. Modeling balloons are very difficult to inflate and cause damage to the lungs or ears if you try to inflate them without a pump.
❖ Do not play with balloons in the kitchen—a balloon may land on a burner or ignited gas ring—or near open fires or radiators.
❖ Dispose of burst balloons immediately by putting them in a wastebasket.

43

How to Make Balloon Balls

Balloon balls are easy and fun to make. They are also very colorful. To start your juggling career you will need three balloon balls.

YOU WILL NEED THESE MATERIALS

Uncooked rice

Scissors

Small plastic bags

Balloons in different colors

1 Cut the stems off two balloons so that you are left with the round part of each balloon. Fill a plastic bag with 1½ cups of rice. Seal in the rice by folding the bag around itself.

2 Insert the bag containing the rice into one of the cut balloons. This is a bit tricky as you have to be careful not to split the bag or the balloon. Do not worry if part of the plastic bag is still visible.

3 Insert the balloon and bag of rice into the second balloon. Make sure the second balloon covers any visible bits of the plastic bag. It does not matter if a part of the first balloon is still visible.

When stretched over the balloon ball, the holes in the outer balloons allow the colors of the balloons beneath to show through. Do not stop now, you have two more balloon balls to make!

4 Cut the stem off another balloon and cut a few small holes into the round part of the balloon. Stretch this balloon over the balloon ball. Repeat using another cut balloon.

How to Make Bean Bags

Get out your sewing thread and needle, it is time to make a juggler's favorite piece of equipment—bean bags!

YOU WILL NEED THESE MATERIALS

Scissors

Uncooked rice

Sewing needle and thread

Remnants of cotton fabric

4 in square of cardboard

Small plastic bags

1 Using the square piece of cardboard as a template, cut out two squares of fabric. To make three bean bags you will need six squares of fabric.

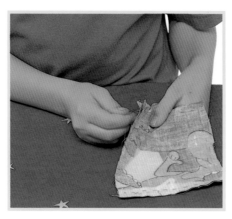

2 Place two squares of fabric right sides facing. Thread the sewing needle and tie a knot at the end of the thread. Sew the squares together along three sides. Turn the fabric bag the right way out.

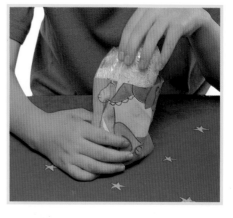

3 Fill the plastic bag with 1 to 2 cups of rice. Seal the plastic bag by wrapping the bag around itself. Place the plastic bag containing the rice inside the fabric bag.

4 Fold over the fabric to make a hem around the opening of the fabric bag. Hold the opening so that the two stitched seams touch, as shown, and sew the edges together, to make a pyramid.

You have now made your first bean bag—only two more to go. Try to use differently patterned or colored fabric for each one. It will make it easier to follow the movement of each bean bag when you start practicing.

One-Ball Workout

Just like an athlete who has to do warm-up exercises before he or she can take to the track, a juggler also goes through a warm-up workout. These moves will help you to become familiar with the weight and shape of the ball, how it moves through the air and how to anticipate where it will fall. Sounds difficult? Not once you have learned the knack. Do this workout every time before a juggling practice session.

YOU WILL NEED

1 juggling ball, balloon ball or bean bag

Handy hint

This workout can be done using all sorts of objects—sneakers, tennis balls, oranges or even elephants (only small ones, of course!). A good juggler can juggle anything, so now is the time to get in some juggling practice.

1 Hold two balls in your right hand. (If you are left-handed, you may want to hold them in your left hand.) Hold one ball in the other hand.

2 Throw the yellow ball in an arc over your head. Keep your eye on the ball and be ready to throw the turquoise ball when the yellow one starts to fall.

3 At this stage the turquoise ball is in mid-air and you have caught the yellow ball. Throw the red ball when the turquoise ball starts to fall.

4 Catch the turquoise ball but keep your eyes on the red ball that is hurtling over your head. Do not look at your hands when they are catching.

5 You can start to breathe again now, for you are about to catch the red ball. Well done—you have successfully completed your first three-ball juggle.

6 **Flashy start**—When you are confident doing steps 1 to 5, try this crowd-pleaser. Hold three balls as in step 1.

7 At the same time throw one ball from each hand straight up. As the balls start to fall, throw the remaining ball in an arc over your head. Keep your eyes on the balls, not your hands.

8 Catch the two balls—one in each hand. When the last ball starts to fall, throw the two balls straight up in the again. Catch the last ball in the opposite hand and then start a normal three-ball juggling routine.

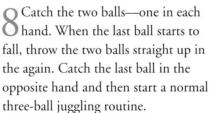

Crazy Juggling

This is a juggling trick for those who really like to perform. You will have to deliver your lines convincingly and look totally embarrassed at the result of your silly trick.

1 Tell your audience that you are going to do an impression of the world's worst juggler. Hold three bean bags in each hand. Then wriggle your body and move your hands about as though you are readying yourself to juggle. Keep looking upward.

3 As soon as the bean bags land—thud, thud, thud—on the floor, make a desperate face and pretend to be upset. You are, after all, the world's worst juggler!

2 The dramatic movement has arrived—throw all six bean bags in the air. Run about waving your arms in the air trying to catch the bags as they fall. Do not catch any bean bags.

Monkey Juggling

No, you are not going to juggle monkeys, only bananas. This trick is as easy as falling out of a tree, but to make it funny you have to get in some silly monkey business.

YOU WILL NEED

3 bananas or bean bags

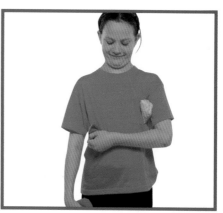

1 Place a bean bag or banana under each arm and hold one in your left hand. Cup your right hand. Release the bean bag tucked under your right arm and catch it smoothly in your right hand while making monkey noises.

2 While still holding the bean bag in your right hand, tuck the bean bag in your left hand under your right arm. As you bring your left arm down, release the bean bag tucked under your left arm.

3 Catch the bean bag in your cupped left hand. Tuck the bean bag held in your right hand under your left arm. As you bring your right arm down, release the bean bag tucked under your right arm.

4 Catch the bean bag in your cupped right hand. Now you start the whole routine again. The aim is to practice this so that you become very quick. By the way, did you keep doing the monkey noises or were you just going bananas?

To really get a laugh, start to swing your arms and lope around the stage like a monkey.

53

Under or Over

This time you are going to juggle three balls under your legs and over your shoulders. What's next—juggling under-water? The important thing with this trick is to raise your leg, rather than bend down. It certainly makes it easier to balance.

YOU WILL NEED

3 juggling balls, balloon balls or bean bags

Handy hint

If you are left-handed, then hold two balls in your left hand and one in your right. Follow the step-by-step instructions, but use your left hand whenever the right hand is mentioned. Likewise, use your right hand when the left is mentioned in the instructions.

Does this boy have three juggling balls growing out of his ears or is his juggling success just going to his head?

1 **Under the leg juggle**—hold two balls in the right hand and one in the left. Raise your right leg, as shown, and get your balance.

2 Put your right hand under your leg and throw the green ball in an arc toward your left hand. Keep watching the ball.

3 While the green ball is in mid-air, throw the blue ball in your left hand in an arc toward your right hand. Catch the green ball in your left hand.

4 Catch the blue ball in your right hand. Continue juggling normally (see Three-Ball Frenzy) except that you will throw the balls from under your leg, not in an arc over your head.

5 **Over the shoulder juggle**—hold two balls in your right hand behind your back. Hold one ball in your left. Look over your shoulder, as shown. Do not stiffen up—try to relax.

6 Throw the yellow ball in your right hand so that it travels upward and then down over your left shoulder. Move your right hand around to the front of your body.

7 When the yellow ball starts to fall, throw the green ball in your left hand in an arc toward your right hand. Catch the yellow ball in your left hand.

8 Catch the green ball in your right hand. Now you can begin to juggle in the normal way, except that you will throw balls over your shoulder.

When you become really good at Under or Over, you can do it with juggling clubs. But be careful that you do not hit yourself on the head!

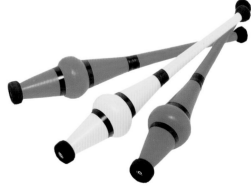

Pampered Pooch

Here we go with your first balloon model. This one should look like a poodle, but do not worry if your first attempt looks more like a bunch of grapes—keep trying!

YOU WILL NEED

Pump

Balloons

1 Inflate and knot a balloon, leaving 4 in uninflated at the end. Starting at the knotted end, twist the balloon to make three 3-in long bubbles. Hold on to the balloon.

2 To form the ears, twist the second and third bubbles around each other. The bubbles are now locked in place. The first bubble forms Pampered Pooch's head and nose.

3 Make three more bubbles slightly larger than the other bubbles. Twist the second and third bubbles around each other to make the front legs.

4 Make three bubbles in the other end of the balloon. The first bubble should be 3 in long, the other two should be slightly larger. Twist together the second and third bubbles to make the hind legs. The bubble nearest the end is pooch's fluffy tail.

To make models of other breeds of dog, like the long-bodied and short-legged dachshund, simply alter the length of the bubbles.

56

Parrot on a Perch

Polly Parrot is a popular bird. When Polly is not on her perch, you can sit her on your head by putting the loop around your chin. No wonder Polly thinks you are crackers!

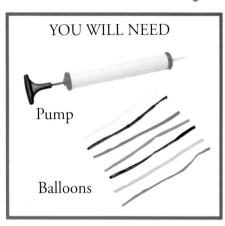

YOU WILL NEED

Pump

Balloons

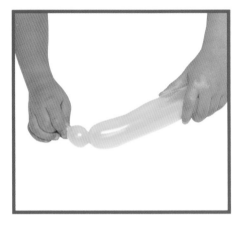

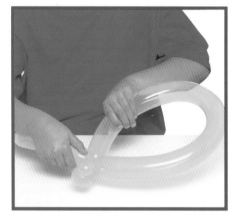

1 Completely inflate a balloon and knot the end. Make a small bubble at the knotted end of the balloon for the parrot's beak.

2 Pull the knot and bubble down beside the rest of the balloon. Twist and lock the knot around the balloon to form another slightly larger bubble. The first bubble is the beak and the second bubble is Polly's head.

3 You will wonder where the next move is leading, but do not worry, it will soon become obvious. Bend the balloon to form a large loop. Twist the balloon around itself about 7 in from the end to make the tail.

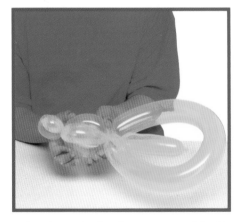

4 This is the hard part, so good luck! Position the tail in the middle of the loop. Pinch and twist the tail and the two sides of the loop together, approximately 3 in below the head, to make the parrot's body and wings. All you need to do now is arrange Polly on her perch.

This parrot on a perch makes a great decoration. Simply tie one end of a piece of string around the top of the perch and attach the other end to your bedroom wall or ceiling.

Big Elephant

Here is an elephant with a great, long trunk. If you want, you can make the ears bigger and the trunk shorter—it will look just as funny!

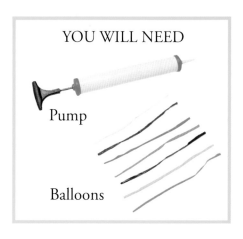

Pump

Balloons

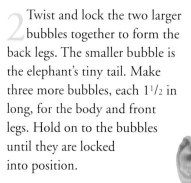

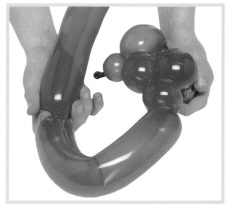

1 To make this balloon model, you start with the tail and work up toward the head. Inflate the balloon, leaving 3 in uninflated at the end. Knot it. Twist the balloon to make three bubbles, the first 1 in long and the next two 1¹/₂ in long.

2 Twist and lock the two larger bubbles together to form the back legs. The smaller bubble is the elephant's tiny tail. Make three more bubbles, each 1¹/₂ in long, for the body and front legs. Hold on to the bubbles until they are locked into position.

3 Twist and lock the end two bubbles to make the front legs. Make two bubbles—one 1 in long and one 4¹/₂ in long—to make the neck and one ear. Twist the long bubble around the small one.

4 Make another 4¹/₂-in bubble. Twist and lock it around the neck bubble. This is the elephant's other ear. Slightly bend the remaining length of balloon to make the enormous, trumpeting trunk.

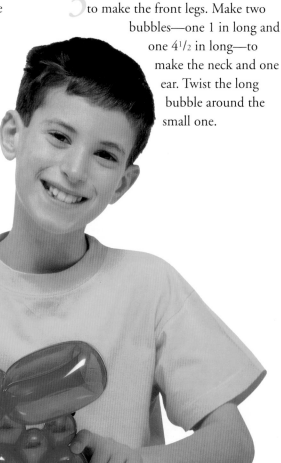

Tiny Mouse

Did you know that elephants are really frightened of mice? Funny to think that something so enormous and strong could be scared of something so tiny and cute.

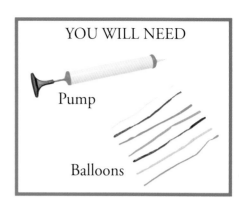
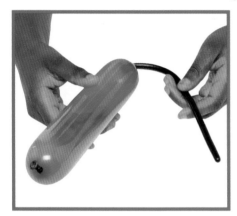

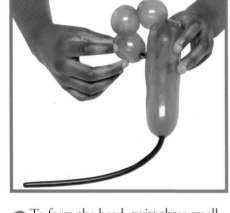

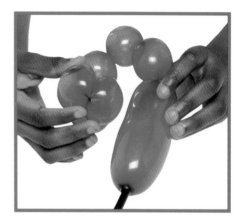

1 To make a tiny mouse, you only need a tiny balloon, so inflate only the first third of the balloon. This will leave the balloon with a long uninflated tail. Tie a knot in the end.

2 To form the head, twist three small bubbles, each 1½ in long. Twist and lock the second and third bubbles together to make the ears. The first bubble forms the head and nose.

3 Twist three small bubbles of the same size to make the neck and front legs. Twist and lock the second and third bubbles as before. See, balloon modeling is easy!

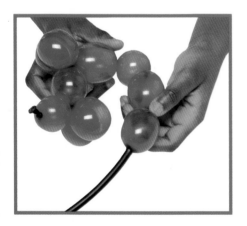

4 Can you guess what comes next? That's right, three more small bubbles! Twist and lock these to form the body and back legs. The rest of the balloon is the mouse's long tail.

Make a family of tiny mice using different colored balloons.

King of Hearts

This smart crown will make you look like the King of Hearts. You do not have to add a balloon to the top of your crown, but why not? You could add a heart-shaped or round balloon, or even some bits of ribbon. Go on and make a crown fit for a king—or queen.

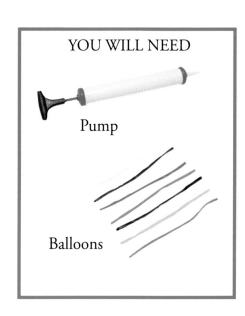

YOU WILL NEED

Pump

Balloons

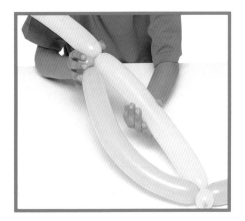

1 Fully inflate two balloons and knot the ends. Twist the balloons together, as shown, to make a headband. The free ends of both balloons should be the same length.

2 Find the midpoint of the free end of each balloon. Twist the two balloons together at the midpoints.

Why not have a balloon hat-making contest to see which of your friends can create the wackiest hat?

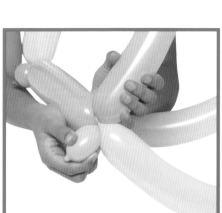

3 Make a small bubble in the end of one free end. Twist it around the headband, halfway along one side.

4 Make a bubble in the other free end. Twist it around the headband, halfway along the opposite side. All loyal subjects should now bow to the king!

Dashing Sword

This Dashing Sword looks great, but it is not much good at cutting anything. At least you and your friends will not hurt each other during mock battles. Make a sheath, or holder, by joining two balloons together and wearing them around your waist.

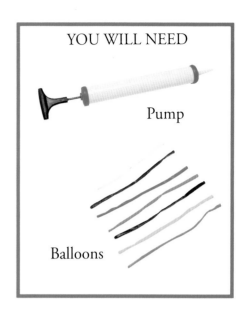

YOU WILL NEED

Pump

Balloons

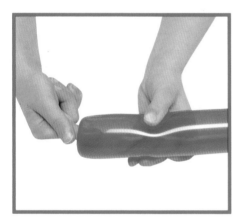

1 Inflate a balloon, leaving 2 in uninflated at the end. Knot the end. Push the knot inside the balloon about 1¹/₂ in and hold it in position. Use your other hand to squeeze the balloon around the knot. Twist the balloon to hold the knot in place.

2 Twist the balloon to make two bubbles. The first bubble will form the handle. The second, longer bubble will form one-third of the shield that protects the hand. Bend the longer bubble, then twist and lock it around the first bubble.

3 Twist the balloon to make another third of the protective hand shield. Twist and lock it around the handle, as before. If you make the hand shield bubbles too long, your Dashing Sword will be really short!

Balloon swords burst very easily, so make your sword fights really gentle or be ready to make lots of swords.

4 Make the final part of the hand shield in the same way.

Crazy Balloon Tricks

Impress and amuse your family and friends with these brilliant balloon stunts. You must never tell anyone the secrets of how to do the tricks.

You are bound to be asked to repeat these tricks, so have a few balloons prepared.

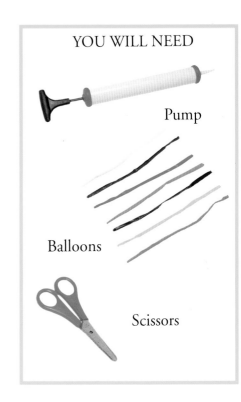

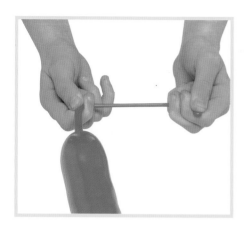

1 **Appearing bubble**—to prepare for this trick, inflate a balloon and leave 7 in uninflated at the end. Knot the balloon. Grip the uninflated section with both hands, as shown. Now stretch the balloon. Go on, really pull!

2 To perform the trick, show the audience that it is an ordinary balloon. Twist a bubble 2 to 3 in long at the end of the balloon and hold it in your hand. The audience should not see you do this.

3 Tell the audience that you will make a bubble appear at the end of the balloon. Without the audience seeing, squeeze the bubble really hard. A small bubble should magically appear at the end of the uninflated section.

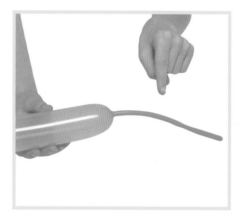

4 **Magic balloon**—to prepare, take two uninflated balloons of the same color and cut the end off one of them with a pair of scissors. Slip the cut-off end onto the end of the whole balloon.

5 Tell your friends you have a magic balloon and offer to show them a trick with it. Inflate the balloon, but leave the end uninflated. There needs to be a space between the real end of the balloon and the false end.

6 Hold the inflated end of the balloon with one hand, and the false end with the other. Say to your friends that the balloon is too long and that you are going to make it shorter. Pull sharply on the false end.

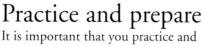

7 Your friends will not understand why the balloon has not deflated.

Practice and prepare

It is important that you practice and prepare these tricks before you perform them in front of an audience. It is also a good idea to figure out exactly what you are going to say.

Do not forget that some of the moves in these tricks are not meant to be seen by the audience.

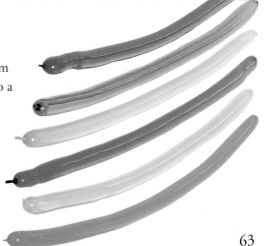

Bunch of Tulips

What a beautiful bunch of tulips! These balloon flowers last longer than real tulips and they do not need watering. You could tie a big, colorful ribbon around the stems to make a lovely present.

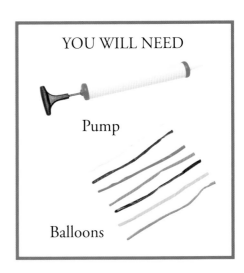

YOU WILL NEED

Pump

Balloons

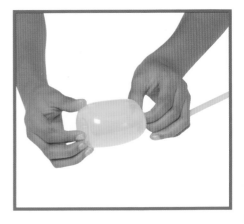

1 Inflate only 3 in of one balloon, leaving a very long uninflated section. This will be the stem of the tulip. Knot the end. Hold the two ends of the inflated section of the balloon, as shown.

2 Use your finger to push the knot into the balloon until the knot reaches the other end of the inflated section. This will take a little bit of practice, so do not give up after the first attempt.

3 Take hold of the knot with the other hand. Remove your finger from inside the balloon. While holding the knot very firmly, twist the balloon several times. This will hold the knot in place.

4 Now that you have made one beautiful tulip, go on to make a whole bunch in different colors.

If you want to be really clever, you can make the tulips stand up by inserting thin plastic straws inside the balloons before you inflate them.

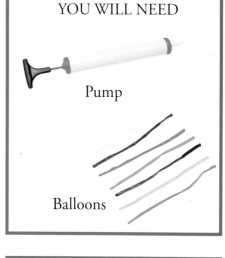

Sunflowers

Just like real sunflowers, these balloon sunflowers are enormous. But unlike the real ones, they will not turn their colorful heads to face the sun. Make two or three and use them to decorate your bedroom.

YOU WILL NEED

Pump

Balloons

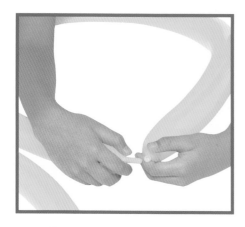

1 Inflate two balloons, leaving only a very short uninflated end in each one. Knot the ends. Tie the knotted end of each balloon to the other end to form two circles.

2 Now for the fun and squeaking. Twist each circle to make a figure eight shape. Both ends of the figure eight should be the same size.

3 Twist the two figure eights together to make a cross. These are the gigantic petals of your sunflower. Let us hope there are no gigantic bees or caterpillars about.

4 Inflate another balloon, once again leaving only a small uninflated end. Twist a loop in the center of the balloon. Twist another loop next to the first one. These are the leaves and stem.

To finish, insert the end of the stem balloon through the center of the petals. Twist the stem to lock it in place.

Building a Balloon House

This house is always popular, and it is really fun to build. Use your imagination to add extra rooms or to make balloon doors, windows, trees, lampposts and furniture. Make it as big as you like, but remember that your house will not be very warm in winter, and you will get soaked when it rains.

YOU WILL NEED

Pump

At least 17 balloons

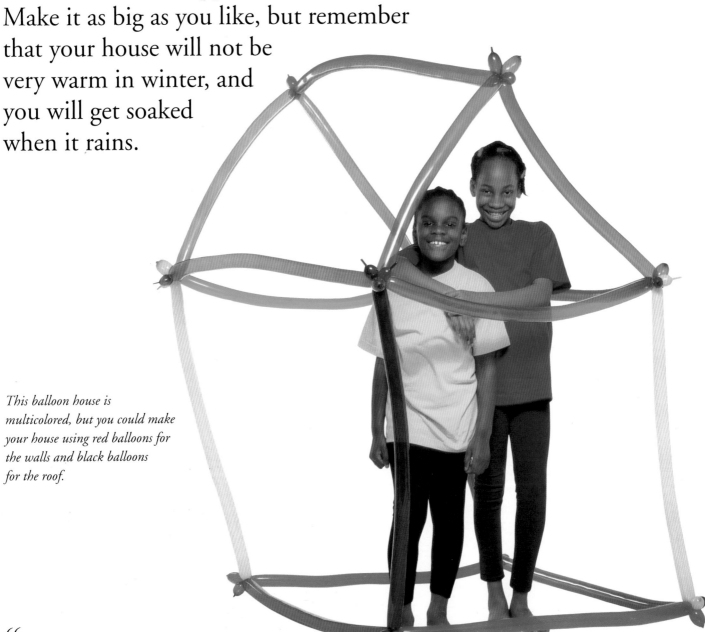

This balloon house is multicolored, but you could make your house using red balloons for the walls and black balloons for the roof.

1 Inflate 17 balloons and knot the ends. Seventeen balloons is enough to build this one-room house, but for grander designs you will need more balloons. Twist the ends of four balloons together to make a square. Make another square in the same way.

2 Use four more balloons to link the two squares together and make a cube. Twist the ends of the balloons to lock them in position. Is it time for a rest yet?

3 Attach a balloon to each top corner of the cube. Twist the end of two balloons together to make a triangle. Do the same with the other two balloons. To finish the roof, link the triangles with a balloon.

4 Well done. You have built a home you can truly call your own. Now is the time to figure out ways of adding extra rooms or making your house a little more private.

Once you have built your first house, go on to create other types of houses. This one is called the lopsided tepee model.

Pop! goes your dream house

Before you start constructing your house, make sure that the floor beneath it is smooth and free of splinters or sharp edges. Sadly, your dream house will collapse if the balloons are punctured. It might be a good idea to cover the building site with an old sheet before you start inflating the balloons.

Bold, Sneaky Tricks

Nick Huckleberry Beak

Introduction

To put on a really amazing magic show you need to know the three Ps. No, not three garden peas, but the three magic Ps—preparation, presentation and performance. You can forget all about that abracadabra mumbo jumbo, just remember the three Ps.

Preparation

To avoid getting halfway through a really clever trick and realizing that you are missing a vital piece of equipment, you must be prepared. You must have everything you will need at your fingertips. The only way that you can be properly prepared is to make a list of the items that are required for each trick. As you gather them together, tick them off the list. Simple idea, but it works. Have you made your list yet? If the answer is no, then get to it!

Presentation

This is all about how you dress and act in front of your audience. Presentation is very important if you want your magic show to be a great success. To find out more about presentation, read Magical style.

Performance

You have decided to put on a show. Congratulations! First thing you must do is figure out which tricks you will do and the order you will do them in. There are no rules for this, but remember that a short show full of great tricks is better than a long show with only a few good tricks.

This trick is in the bag (or should that be envelope?) because this girl has everything prepared.

The best way to give your magic show atmosphere is to use music. Try to match the speed and mood of the music to the pace and style of your act. If you are doing lots of quick tricks, use fast music. If your show is spooky and full of shocking surprises, find a piece of really creepy music.

If you do not use music then you will have to write a script and rehearse the words you are going to say. You may want to introduce each magic trick or tell a little story about where you learned a certain trick. But whatever you say, it is a good idea to have prepared it. It also never hurts to have a couple of good jokes up your sleeve. These can be used to entertain your audience while you get your next trick ready. Do not use any bad jokes—only I am allowed to use them.

Magical style

Even if you can do some of the hardest magic tricks in the world, your show might flop if your presentation style is dead boring. To be a big hit with an audience you have to have pizzazz, you have to have style. Problem is, you cannot buy pizzazz at a supermarket (I tried once and came out with two frozen pizzas instead), but you can learn the tricks of great presentation.

Make a big show of displaying empty hands or objects to your audience. It will distract them from seeing what you are really up to!

This boy has magical style. He is smiling, wearing his favorite hat and looks ready to take a big bow.

My last tip to you is this—let the audience know you have finished a trick by taking a small bow. Save the big bow until the end. As soon as they see you bow, the audience will clap and call out for more.

Entertaining style

This one is easy to explain. If you have a smile on your face and look as though you are enjoying what you are doing, the audience will also enjoy themselves. Try to look confident and relaxed. When you talk to your audience, speak clearly and loudly. No one will hear your great jokes if you mumble and mutter.

Professional style

If the audience asks you to repeat a trick or to tell them how it was done, refuse politely. If you tell all your secrets, you will have to learn a whole new routine, and a trick is never as good the second time around.

Sometimes it helps to look as surprised as your audience.

Dress style

The traditional costume for a magician is a smart suit, bow tie and flashy cape. Nowadays almost any sort of costume is fine. A colorful shirt and a pair of jeans can look just as eye-catching and professional. If you want to find your own wacky costume, go ahead. My rule is—if you feel good, you will look good.

Stage style

To be a show-stopping performer, you must know the secrets of the trade. The first is, always enter from the side or from the back of the stage. Then walk to the middle, smile at your audience and wait for the applause.

The second thing to do is to introduce yourself to the audience. You can use your own name or invent a snazzy-sounding stage name.

Number three is always to face your audience. This will mean that your props, or equipment, will have to be within easy reach. Your audience has not come to watch you rummage in a box.

The fourth trade secret is this—if you make a mistake or a trick does not work, try to laugh it off. You can even pretend that the mistake was meant to happen. Then you can do the trick again, but this time do it correctly.

Materials

These are some of the main materials and items of equipment you will need.

Carbon paper When placed between two sheets of paper, inky side down, it will copy whatever is written on the top sheet of paper.

Colored and white paper and cardboard For many of the projects, you can recycle pieces of paper and use cardboard from cut-up cereal boxes. Large sheets of cardboard can be bought at stationery and craft stores.

Contact paper This plastic material comes in many colors and designs. It is usually bought in rolls. To make it adhere to a surface, you simply peel off the protective backing and press the contact paper onto the object.

Marker A marker is a type of felt-tip pen that draws quite thick lines. If you do not have a marker, use an ordinary felt-tip pen instead.

Paper clips A good collection of paper clips is vital for any promising magician.

Recycled boxes For the projects in this book, you will need two empty boxes—a large one and a small one. A cereal box and a small tea or chocolate box would be ideal.

Rubber bands These are almost as important to the budding magician as paper clips. You can buy bags of assorted rubber bands at stationery stores.

Ruler Accurate measuring is required for some projects, so you will need a ruler divided into inches (in).

Safety scissors Safety scissors are smaller than cutting scissors. Their edges are rounded and the blades are not as sharp as normal scissors.

String It does not matter if you use plain or colored string as long as you have lots of it.

White glue This is a strong glue that can be used to stick together paper, wood or even fabric. It can be bought at stationery stores and is sometimes called craft glue. You will need a brush or glue spreader to apply the glue.

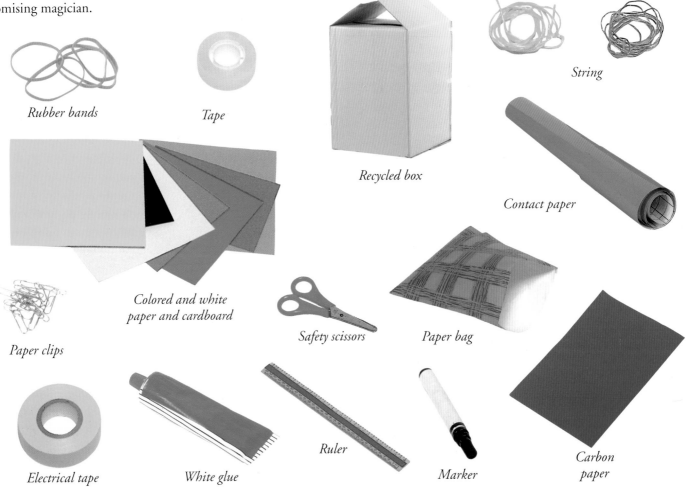

Rubber bands

Tape

String

Recycled box

Contact paper

Colored and white paper and cardboard

Paper clips

Safety scissors

Paper bag

Electrical tape

White glue

Ruler

Marker

Carbon paper

Equipment

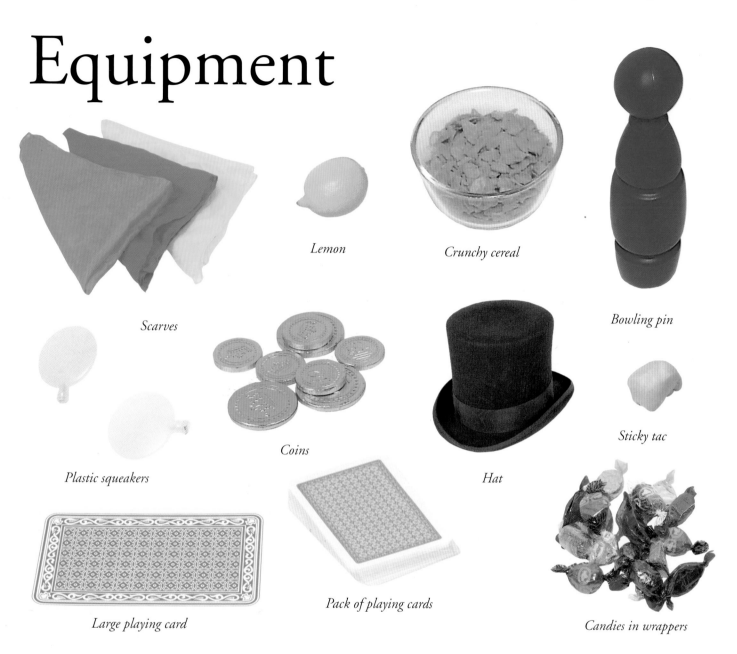

Scarves

Lemon

Crunchy cereal

Bowling pin

Plastic squeakers

Coins

Hat

Sticky tac

Large playing card

Pack of playing cards

Candies in wrappers

Bowling pin This is used when playing indoor or lawn bowling. It is made of plastic.

Candies in wrappers You will need quite a few candies wrapped in foil or cellophane. Do not start eating them before you have completed the trick!

Coins You can use real or plastic toy money when practicing or performing tricks. You will need five coins.

Crunchy cereal Use a breakfast cereal made of large, crunchy flakes. Ask permission before raiding the kitchen!

Hat All magicians have got to have a hat—your audience will expect it! It can be a dashing top hat, a favorite baseball cap or even a crazy sun hat.

Large playing card This is about four times the size of a normal playing card. You can buy a large playing card at joke and toy stores.

Lemon You can use a real or plastic lemon to perform the Magic Box trick.

Plastic squeakers These are round, plastic discs that squeak when squeezed. You can buy them at joke and toy stores. They are not expensive.

Playing cards A pack of playing cards consists of 52 cards plus two jokers. There are four suits—hearts, diamonds, clubs and spades—numbered from ace to king. There are two black suits and two red suits. To do all the tricks you will need two packs of cards. Playing cards are inexpensive and can be bought at toy and stationery stores.

Scarves You can use large or small silky scarves or handkerchiefs. Brightly colored or patterned ones are best.

Sticky tac This reusable material is used to hold posters onto walls. You can buy it in packs at stationery stores.

Missing Money

This trick is every magician's favorite. Why? Because it cannot go wrong. All you need are five coins and some tape attached to the palm of your hand. Keep the palm of your hand hidden throughout the trick, otherwise the audience will figure out your secret.

Handy hint

In place of a loop of tape you can use a small piece of double-sided tape. Use small coins rather than large ones—large coins are harder to conceal and too heavy to adhere to the tape. You can use plastic coins if you like.

YOU WILL NEED THESE MATERIALS

5 small coins of the same size

Strong, clear tape

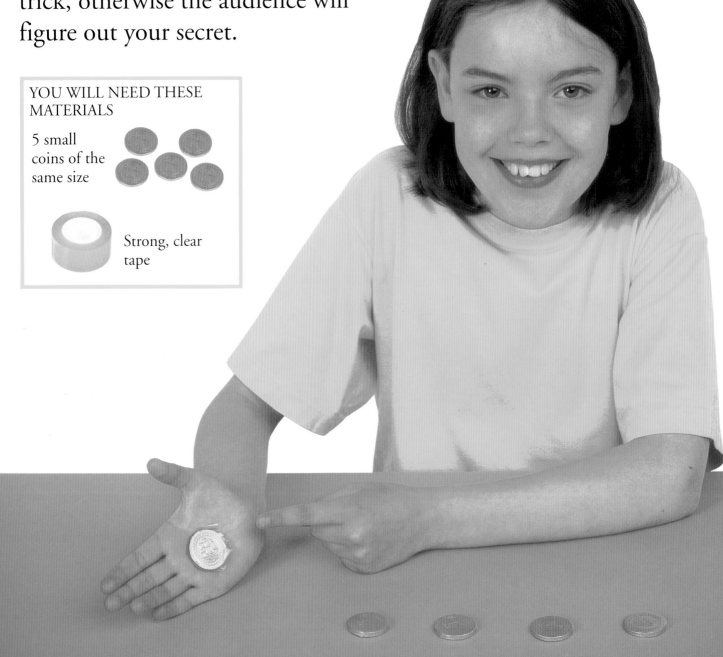

1 Cut a small piece of tape about 2 in long. Overlap the ends, sticky side out, to make a loop. Place the five coins in front of you on the table.

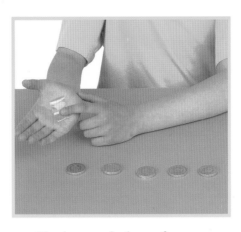

2 Firmly press the loop of tape onto the palm of your hand. Do not let anyone see you doing this. This little bit of magical sneakiness is just between you and me.

3 Make a big show of counting the five coins one-by-one as you stack them neatly one on top of the other. Ask your audience to count along with you.

4 Press the hand with the sticky loop onto the pile of coins. Say your chosen magic words and then withdraw your hand. The top coin will be stuck to the loop.

5 Keep the palm concealing the coin flat on the table. With the other hand, spread out the pile of coins and count them out loud. Yikes! There are now only four coins.

It is a secret!

In this trick, the missing coin remains missing. You do not reveal where you have concealed the fifth coin. Remove the coin and tape from your hand discreetly while you are returning the other coins to your pocket or to your magic box.

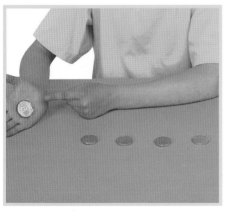

6 The fifth coin, of course, is still stuck to your hand.

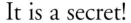

Tricky Tubes

This is another classic trick that is used by magicians everywhere. It involves moving a handkerchief from one "magic" tube to another tube to give the impression that both tubes are empty. In the finalé of this trick you stun the audience by producing a handkerchief from the empty tubes.

YOU WILL NEED THESE MATERIALS

2 pieces of different colored cardboard 12 in x 12 in

Rubber band

Small handkerchief

9 paper clips

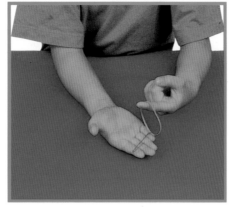

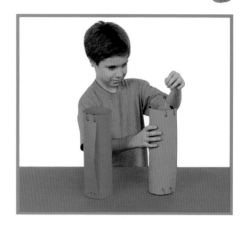

1 Steps 1, 2 and 3 show what you have to do to prepare for this trick. Roll the pieces of cardboard to make tubes. One tube must be narrower so that it will fit inside the larger tube. Secure the tubes with eight paper clips.

2 The device that makes this trick work is a paper clip. Unfold the paper clip to make hooks at each end, as shown. Attach a rubber band to one hook. Roll up the handkerchief and thread it into the rubber band.

3 Hook the other end of the paper clip onto the top of the narrow tube. The rubber band and the handkerchief will be on the inside of the tube. Make sure that the handkerchief is totally hidden from view.

4 Now it is time to get this show on the road. Hold up the large tube so that the audience can see that it is completely empty. This should not be difficult, as it really is empty.

5 Pick up the narrow tube and slide it slowly down through the large tube. As you do this the paper clip holding the handkerchief will hook itself onto the large tube.

6 Pull the narrow tube out from the bottom of the large tube. Then, with a flourish, hold up the narrow tube to show your audience that it is empty.

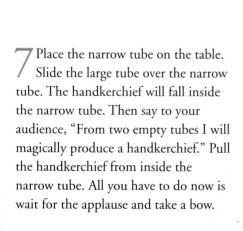

7 Place the narrow tube on the table. Slide the large tube over the narrow tube. The handkerchief will fall inside the narrow tube. Then say to your audience, "From two empty tubes I will magically produce a handkerchief." Pull the handkerchief from inside the narrow tube. All you have to do now is wait for the applause and take a bow.

Magic Box

The Magic Box can produce objects out of thin air. One minute the box is empty, the next it is not. Only you know about the secret box that can hold a lemon, a deck of cards or even an elephant. If you are going to pull an elephant out of the box, perhaps this trick should be called the Magic Trunk!

Practice makes perfect

To get this trick right takes lots of practice. You should be so familiar with it that the audience is not even aware that you turn the box around in step 8. One wrong move and the lemon (or the elephant) will come tumbling out for all the world to see. To make this trick really impressive, ask someone in the audience to lend you their watch, wallet or sunglasses. Their mouth will drop when they see their object disappear and then reappear.

YOU WILL NEED THESE MATERIALS

1 small recycled box

1 large recycled box

Tape

Ruler

Scissors

Marker

White glue

Lemon

Contact paper

1 To make the Magic Box, tape the ends of the boxes closed. Cut the top off the small box. Use the marker and ruler to draw a line along one long and two short edges of the large box.

2 Cut along these lines carefully to make a hinged lid on the large box. By the way, did I tell you to empty the boxes before you started this project? Oops, oh well.

3 Do the same to the other side of the large box, but this time the hinged lid is on the opposite edge. You must get this right or the Magic Box will not be very magical.

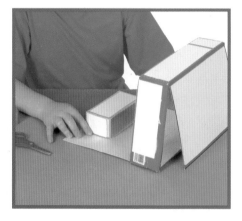

4 Tape, glue or nail the small box securely to the inside of one of the hinged lids. (Forget nailing—I was just joking.) The opened top of the small box must face where the lid is hinged.

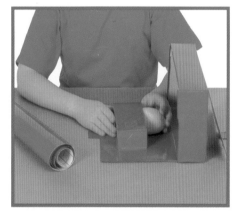

5 Cover the box with contact paper. Cut two strips of this paper to make tabs. Attach tabs to the outside edge of the lids, fold in half and tape to the inside edge. Put the lemon in the small box.

6 Now it is magic time. Place the box on the table. The lid containing the small box is on the bottom with the tab nearest you. Hold on to both tabs because you are about to open the box.

7 Raise the box and pull on the tabs to open both lids. Say to your audience, "This box is empty—but not for long." Lay the box on the table.

8 The lid containing the lemon should be on the bottom. Turn the box around, hold the tab and lift the lid. Hold up the lemon to the audience.

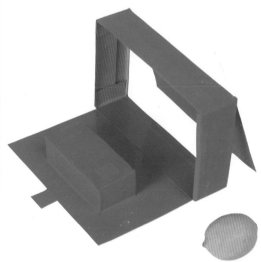

79

The Big Picture

So that you can say hello or farewell to your audience in a magical way, I have prepared this special trick. It is a very simple illusion where a small picture suddenly becomes a big picture. Carefully follow the instructions for folding the paper, or you will be saying hello or goodbye to yourself.

This is how the trick starts. You show the small picture, then, with a quick flick of your wrist, it suddenly becomes The Big Picture!

1 To prepare for this trick, place a sheet of paper with a long side nearest you. Draw a large picture of someone waving on the paper. Keep the drawing simple; you will have to repeat it later.

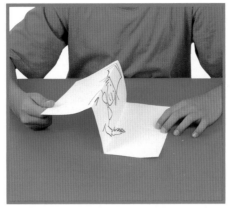

2 Turn the paper so that the picture is upside-down. Fold the paper accordian-style, making the right-hand flap larger than the other two. The right-hand flap is on the bottom, as shown.

3 Fold the paper away from you, so that the top flap is a little smaller than the bottom flap. I know this sounds complicated, but it is easy. I could not do it if it was too hard.

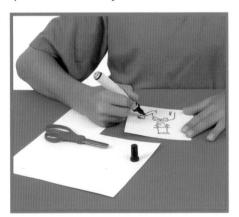

4 Take the other sheet of paper and cut out a rectangle that is exactly the same size as the bottom flap of the folded paper. On this rectangle, draw the picture that is on the folded paper.

5 Glue this picture onto the front of the large flap. The bottom of the picture will be nearest the fold. (See, I told you this is easy!) Apply the glue carefully so that it does not spread onto the other flaps. You are ready to present The Big Picture.

6 Hold the paper, as shown, with the fold at the bottom and the small drawing facing the audience. To keep the paper from unfolding, support the flap with a little finger. Tell the audience that you are going to give them a cheery welcome or a sad farewell wave.

7 Quickly pull sideways so that the folded paper unfolds and The Big Picture is revealed.

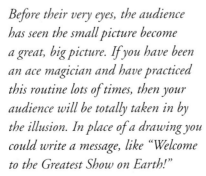

Before their very eyes, the audience has seen the small picture become a great, big picture. If you have been an ace magician and have practiced this routine lots of times, then your audience will be totally taken in by the illusion. In place of a drawing you could write a message, like "Welcome to the Greatest Show on Earth!"

The Big Card Trick

You may have seen this trick performed many times, but now you will be able to do it yourself. You can choose any number or suit you want for the large playing card, but a card of the same number and suit must be at the top of your deck of playing cards. The two cards attached to the large card must be numerically smaller than the big card.

YOU WILL NEED THESE MATERIALS

Deck of playing cards and 1 large envelope

Sticky tac

Large playing card

Handy hint

You can make your own large playing card with white cardboard and a black marker. It does not matter which suit or number you choose to draw, as long as it is the same as the top card on your deck of cards.

1 To prepare for this trick, use a small piece of sticky tac to attach a two and a four of any suit onto the back of the large ten of clubs card. Place them in the envelope. Also check that the ten of clubs is the top card on your deck of playing cards. Now let the show begin.

2 Invite someone from the audience to join you on stage and cut the deck of cards. No, not with a pair of scissors. To cut the cards, all your guest has to do is take a pile of cards off the top of the deck and lay them beside the remaining cards.

3 Place the bottom half of the deck on top of the other cards. Place it so that it is at right angles to the cut cards. This will show you where the deck was cut and where you will find the ten of clubs. Tell your guest that they will shortly see their secret card.

4 Remove the upper stack of cards from the pile and turn over the next card. Without looking at the card, show it to your guest. Tell them that they must remember what their secret card is. You know that it is the ten of clubs!

5 Ask your guest to shuffle the cards as much as they like. When they are shuffled, you can put them into the envelope. This envelope contains the large ten of clubs card plus the two other smaller cards.

6 Tell your guest that you are going to find their secret card. Put your hand into the envelope and pull out the two card. Ask if this is the secret card. They will say no. You then ask, "Is it bigger than this?"

7 Repeat the routine as in step 6, but this time pull out the four card. It is now your big moment to astound and amuse everyone. Put your hand into the envelope again and pull out the large ten of clubs card. Show it to your guest and say, "Is this big enough?" You have shown your guest that you knew that their chosen card was the ten of clubs all the time.

See the Unseen

Here are two techniques for seeing the unseen—reading messages that you were never intended to read. For the first method you have to get hold of the notepad quickly.

YOU WILL NEED THESE MATERIALS

Notepad

Wax crayon

Carbon paper

Scissors

1 **Method 1**—Get the notepad on which the torn-out message was written. Rub the crayon gently over the top sheet. The impression made by the written message will remain unshaded.

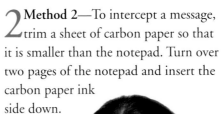

2 **Method 2**—To intercept a message, trim a sheet of carbon paper so that it is smaller than the notepad. Turn over two pages of the notepad and insert the carbon paper ink side down.

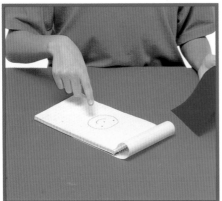

3 Once the message has been written and the person is out of sight, turn the top pages of the notepad over and remove the carbon paper. On the page below will be a copy of the message. Take care doing this and never attempt to intercept truly personal messages.

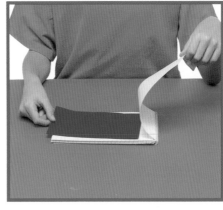

Noisy Alarms

Crunch, crackle, pop, squeak! What are those noises? They are the sounds of your bedroom security devices going noisily into action. I bet the intruder got a surprise!

Handy hint

You will have to keep changing the positions of your alarms or they will prove ineffective against intruders.

1 **Noisy warning 1**—This may sound a little odd, but crunchy cereal makes a great nighttime alarm. All you have to do is leave a pile of cereal just outside your bedroom door.

2 When the unwitting intruder steps on the cereal, you will hear the crunch, crackle and pop! The intruder will realize that their sneaky game is up and will run away.

3 **Noisy warning 2**—In case the intruder misses the crunchy cereal alarm, place one plastic squeaker under a rug near the door and another under the cushion of a chair. (Even intruders have to sit down sometime!) Now all you have to do is wait.

When you hear the squeakers "squeak" you will know that you have not caught a mouse, but a sneaky rat!

Trick Wallet

Open one flap of this wallet and it is empty. Open it the other way and—wow!—there is the secret document. Make two identical Trick Wallets so that you and a friend can switch wallets (and secret information) without being detected. When using the wallet to play a trick on someone, distract his or her attention so that they do not notice you turning the wallet over.

Handy hint

If you are going to use your Trick Wallet as part of a magic act, the wallet should be quite large. This will make it easier for the audience to see what is and what is not happening. When using the wallet for secret messages, make sure it will fit easily into a pocket.

YOU WILL NEED THESE MATERIALS

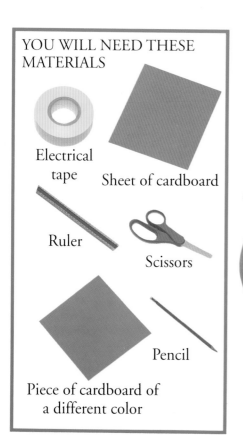

Electrical tape

Sheet of cardboard

Ruler

Scissors

Pencil

Piece of cardboard of a different color

1 Measure and draw three rectangles, each 8 in x 3 in onto the sheet of cardboard. Cut out the rectangles. You can make a big wallet by cutting out three larger rectangles.

2 Lay the rectangles side by side and join the edges with electrical tape, as shown. The tape should act like a hinge, allowing each piece of cardboard to fold over easily.

3 Tape the seams on the back of the cardboard and place electrical tape along the remaining two short sides. Position the tape so that it can be folded over to the back to give a neat finish.

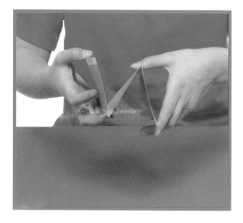

4 Accordian-fold the wallet, as shown. Lay the wallet onto the table and gently press it flat.

5 To test the Trick Wallet, place a small rectangle of the other colored cardboard between two of the flaps. Close the flaps. Turn the wallet over and open the flap. If the flap is empty you are doing the right thing. Close this flap.

Magic trick wallet

To make the wallet work in a magic show routine, you have to be discreet when turning the wallet over so that your audience does not catch onto the trick. The only way to achieve this sleight of hand is to distract them by making a funny face or telling a joke. A good magician always has (among other things!) a couple of good jokes up his or her sleeve.

6 Turn the wallet over again and open the flap. If all has gone to plan, the flap will contain the piece of cardboard.

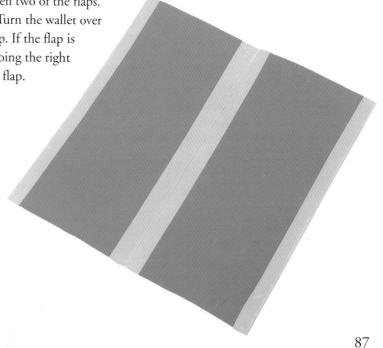

Joke in the Mail

Want to send someone a shocking surprise? All it takes is paper, paper clips and tape. Joke in the Mail is so easy to assemble that you could make one for each of your friends. But will they still be your friends after you have played this joke on them?

YOU WILL NEED THESE MATERIALS

1 small envelope

Tape

Sheet of paper or thin cardboard

2 small rubber bands

3 paper clips

Marker

1 Fold the sheet of paper or thin cardboard into equal thirds. Press the folds flat with your hands and then open out the paper again.

2 Open out two paper clips to make L-shapes, as shown. Bend and shape another paper clip to form a circle. Do this carefully—the ends are sharp.

3 Tape the L-shaped paper clips to the paper and loop rubber bands around the ends, as shown. Thread the rubber bands onto the wire circle.

4 Slowly wind the wire circle around and around. The rubber bands will twist and tighten. Whatever you do, do not let go.

5 Re-fold the paper without letting go of the wire circle. Carefully insert the folded paper into the envelope and seal the envelope.

6 Address the envelope using the marker. Mail or hand-deliver the envelope to your friend.

7 When your friend opens the letter the rubber bands will unwind, causing the wire circle to spin and clatter against the paper. This is bound to make your friend jump in fright.

Handy Signals

Getting messages to friends can be tricky when you are involved in a hush-hush surveillance operation or working in the library. So instead of shouting messages, use hand signals. On the next page are examples of just a handful (ha, ha!) of hand signals and their meanings. Use them alone to convey a simple message or link them together for more complicated instructions. When you have mastered these signals, go on to invent your own.

YOU WILL NEED

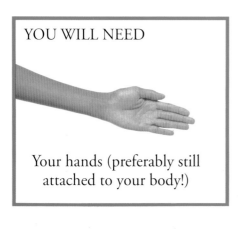

Your hands (preferably still attached to your body!)

1 **Quiet!**—Press a finger to your lips when you want someone to stop talking. Move the finger over to your ear to say "listen."

2 **Yes and no**—Resting your chin on a hand with the thumb pointing up means "yes." To say "no," point the thumb down.

3 **Danger warning**—Place a hand loosely around your throat to warn friends that the situation is dangerous and to take care.

4 **Come here**—Running a hand through your hair from the front to the back means "come here."

5 **Go away**—Hiding your face behind one hand means "go away." Use two hands to say "go away quickly."

6 **Look**—Placing a finger next to the right eye means "look right." A finger next to the left eye means "look left." Fingers next to both eyes means "look straight ahead."

When you have mastered these signals, go on and invent your own. But before you forget what each new signal means, write it down.

Bold, Sneaky Tricks FINAL CHALLENGE

Final Challenge

Your mission is to rescue the bowling pin from the circle using only string and a rubber band. You and your accomplice cannot enter the circle nor touch the pin. The only piece of floor the pin can touch is the area on which it is standing. Good luck!

YOU WILL NEED THESE MATERIALS

Scissors

Rubber band

Balls of string

Plastic bowling pin

The Final Challenge is not easy, but that makes it all the more challenging. Now it is time to put your thinking caps on—there is a poor lonely bowling pin in distress that needs to be rescued.

1 Draw a circle 4 ft in diameter using the chalk. (A hoop is used here for clarity). Place the bowling pin in the middle of the circle. Cut four lengths of string 2 yd long.

2 Thread lengths of string through the rubber band. The rubber band should be midway along each string. Hold the ends of the strings, as shown.

3 Gently pull on the strings to stretch the rubber band so that it will fit easily over the top of the bowling pin. Lower the rubber band over the neck of the pin.

4 Allow the rubber band to tighten around the pin by relaxing your pull on the strings. Carefully raise the pin out of the circle. Do not pull on the strings, as this will loosen the rubber band's grip on the pin.

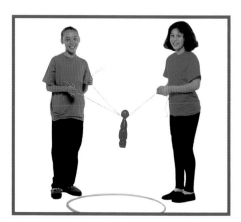

5 Congratulations, you have done it! Now see if your friends can do it.

This is a great game to play at a party. To make it more difficult for your friends, you can set a time limit in which the challenge must be completed.

93

Index

Acknowledgments

The publishers would like to thank the following children for appearing in this book, and of course their parents:
Nana Addae, Richard Addae, Michelle Apeagyei, Steve Jason Aristizabal, Joshua Ashford, Rula Awad,
Nadia el-Ayadi, Nicola Barnard, Michael Bewley, Emma Blue, Leah Bone, Cerys Brunsdon, William Carabine,
Alexander Clare, Emma Cotton, Charli Coulson, Laurence Defraitus, Alaba Fashina, Fiona Fulton,
Nicola Game, Lana Green, Laura Harris-Stewart, Jonathan Headon, Gerald Ishiekwene, Stella-Rae James,
Aribibia Johnson, Reece Johnson, Carl Keating, Camille Kenny-Ryder, Lee Knight, Kevin Lake, Barry Lee,
Kirsty Lee, Isaac John Lewis, Alex Lindblom-Smith, Scott Longstaff, Laura Masters, Claire McCarthy,
Erin McCarthy, Trevor Meechan, Hugh Hong Mo, Jessica Moxley, Lucy Nightingale, Ify Obi, Adenike Odeleye,
Wura Odurinde, Laurence Ody, Abayomi Ojo, Fola Oladimeji, Ola Olawe, Michael Oloyede, Yemisi Omolewa,
Tope Oni, Josephina Quayson, Pedro Henrique Queiroz, Jamie Rosso,
Nida Sayeed, Charlie Simpson, Justine Spiers, Nicola Twiner, Sarah Twiner,
Frankie David Viner, Nhat Han Vong, Devika Webb, Tanel Yusef.

Contributors: Nick Huckleberry Beak and Hugh Nightingale.

Gratitude also to Hampden Gurney School, Walnut Tree Walk
Primary School and St John the Baptist Church of England School.

The authors would like to thank the following for their assistance in
providing materials and advice:

Boots; Dylon Consumer Advice; Head Gardener, Knightsbridge; Lady
Jayne; Mason Pearson, Kent; Molton Brown; Tesco. Special thanks to
Justin of Air Circus; "Smiley Face" from Theater Crew, Tunbridge
Wells; and the Bristol Juggling Convention.